POISON AND ANTIDOTE

SAMYUKTA B

To my mom, for teaching me the way of life

To my dad, for inspiring me

Contents

Acknowledgements

This book couldn't have been possible without the help of my parents.

My mother, Shashirekha, is my best friend and guide. She taught me so much about life and its realities, which inspired this book in me. She also helped in editing it.

I thank my dad, Balasubramanian, for always believing in me and my abilities. He has been a great support throughout the process of making this book and has helped me in coming up with creative poem titles.

I need to thank my friend, Prithviraj, for being very appreciative of and enthusiastic about my poems. He has constantly motivated me to write and insisted that my poems are relatable.

And finally, my college friends, Bhavya, Sathya, Safiya, Harshith, Riya, Sanjay, Lohith and Smaran have been encouraging and supportive of my work. I express my gratitude here. I know I have you all as readers to write for.

Preface

The first poetry piece I wrote was in September 2020. I noticed that people usually wrote about something they have experienced strongly in their personal life. I penned down my thoughts and feelings about a toxic friendship I was dealing with, at that time. It was a personal piece.

Once I had written it down, I realized that I was not troubled by those emotions anymore. This helped bring a sense of closure to the situation. I realized that poetry can be therapeutic and also working with the flow of words can be fun. That's how my poetic journey began.

Once I put together a few pieces, I opened up an Instagram account for poetry. There, I met many talented poets and writers. It felt very inspiring and encouraging to be part of the group. There were so many followers ready to support my creative work. Being part of the poetic community really helped boost my imagination and creative skills and I surprised myself with the different themes that I came up with.

I had been into writing prose for a long time but there is something different about penning down an emotion in verse. It started growing into a beautiful experience to the point that I realized that it wouldn't be just a passing hobby. Poetry would always be part of my life.

I was going through a lot of changes in my life - learning about people, choices and mistakes, discovering the dualities of life - the light and the dark side, good people and fake friends, growth, and failure. I decided that this would be the theme of my book.

I loved every moment of writing this book and drawing every one of the illustrations. The poems in this book are very dear to me because they are experiences that I have gone through or that my loved ones have.

I have written this book with a desire to share my journey of life, with the hope that it will touch and inspire every reader in some way. I hope these verses speak to you.

1. Into the Abyss

Poison

The poison takes its slow course
meandering its way through my veins.
It reaches up to my soul
to find it strangled in pain.
There's a war going on
with my fears and worries standing guard
Confidence has been locked behind bars
The room for positivity has been burnt to the ground
The feeling of hope is nowhere to be found
Self-doubt and uncertainty don't let anyone through
Strength and courage are cowering in a corner
Poison engulfs my entire heart.
But now I'm immune to its toxin
It won't let me leave
Now I'm stuck in this world
where everyone grows their own poison trees.

Pillow Thoughts

Lying awake at night
disturbed by those weary thoughts
that refuse to leave my mind
I think about the things
that I shouldn't have said
and of all the issues to which it has led.
There's nothing I could possibly do now
except close my eyes and just lie there.

Cul-de-sac

She was lost so deep
in the maze of her own worries
there was no right or left
and the straight path was a dead end.

Can't face reality

My mind feels numb
and strangely silent
like a hush that descends
before an upcoming storm.
I'm closing the curtains
and shutting the doors
on everything around me
I don't have the courage
to face reality.

Compass

I'm lost and afraid
so many choices to make.
Will the compass of my soul
show me the right way?

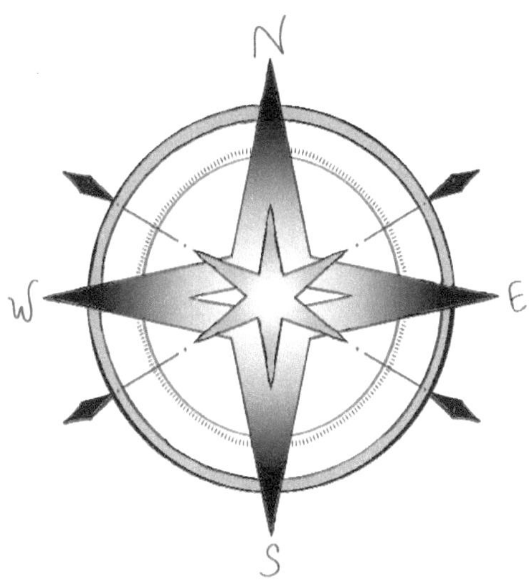

The Monster Inside

The monster under her bed
didn't give her much dread.
The one she saw in the mirror
was the demon she feared.

Weight of my Sins

Sins of the past haunt me in my sleep
regrets and faults that can't be undone.
Do I drown in the misery of my guilty soul?
or do I close my eyes so I can't wake up anymore?

Into a Dark Hole

All that I've worked hard for
has gone in vain.
Anguish and frustration
are the only things that remain.
There's a dark hole in the ground
which is deep and cold.
I just want to get inside
and be away from this world.

Silent nights

In the silent nights when thoughts are loudest,
the whispers of the wind are no comfort
I recollect those dreadful feelings
and I wonder when the gloom will pass.

Mine to carry

There's a load on my head
I can't think properly.
There's a burden on my shoulder
I can't put it down lightly.

Déjà vu

Standing over the precipice
with the taste of death on my lips
I hear the deafening silence
in the void of my thoughts.
I look down at the abyss
anticipating the cosmic view.
As my life flashes before me
I get an intense feeling of déjà vu.

Not my Script

I have a script in my hand
but I don't think it belongs to me.
They force me to stand on the stage
and read it out loudly
so they can watch me
struggle with my lines.
Did I ever have a script of my own?
I don't remember
Now I'm stuck in this play
they won't let me improvise.

Toxicity

Why do I do things
for people who don't deserve it?
Why do I go out of my way
when they don't even care a bit?
Why do I love them
despite their toxicity?
Should I just leave
or wait unitl they reciprocate?

Not so cool

We were on the same side
I trusted you with all I had
we mutually agreed to be bosom friends.
Now, in the blink of an eye
I see you standing on the other side
with those people you call 'cool'.
You sold my secrets
and made fun of me.
When they cheered you on
you thought it was 'cool'.
Now, you have lost a good friend
I would have been with you till the end.
And they have left you all alone saying
you were a terrible friend.

Strings Unsewn

You pulled at my heartstrings,
one by one,
until you had threads of love
unfurled in your hands
but you forgot to sew them back.

Left behind scars

Beneath these scars
lie a hundred stories
of pain and hurt
that you never cared to know
and why would you,
you left some, on your own.

Comforts of a Lie

You strung words
carefully into sentences
hoping I wouldn't notice
the lies in between.
It might have pained my ears
but they weren't closed.
The unpleasant truth
is what you tried to bury
but through that
your faithless self
you revealed.

Backstabbing

The blood on my back
is a sign of betrayal
and the death of a friendship.
The trust and secrets lie
shattered on the floor
and you stamp on those pieces
and walk out the door.

Hurt Concealed

You can't see what I won't show you
maybe, I'll hide my wounds
and you'll never know.

2. Under the Dark Clouds

Locker

Darling, what are you doing?
You take every piece of sadness
and hide it inside the locker
bury the key under the ground
so you never have to feel it.
You brush the hurt
under the carpet
so you never have to accept
what lies beneath it.
You build up a stone wall
against your fears
turn your head around
and close your ears.
You keep a hankie ready
to wipe away the tears
and put on a smile
for everyone to see.
Do you think
that this is healthy?
Why do you think
expressing sadness is weak?
Why do you close the doors
on things that need attention?
Why do you procrastinate

feeling unhappiness?
Why do you order yourself
to forget the past?

Hurt you've kept shut

That door is a mystery
only you know what's behind it.
How will it open
if it is locked
and you've lost the key?

Denial

Everything happens for a reason
do you ever stop to think why?
You might always view the glass as half full
never bothering to think otherwise.
Your eyes are on the butterflies in your garden
but you don't want to look at the weeds.
You avoid the roses with thorns
and pick up the dandelions instead.
Living your entire life in denial
isn't going to get you out of your woes.
Sometimes you will have to face the dark clouds
and you just might not have a raincoat.

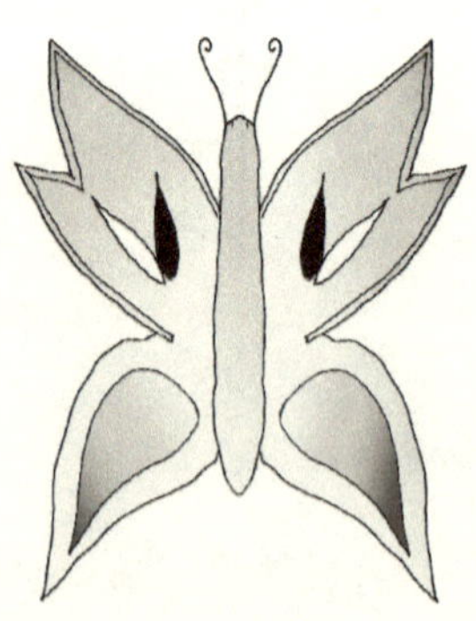

Accept

Feel the tears rolling down your cheek
sense the flush as you weep
close your eyes and let the pain flow
accept that what was is no more.

They're not coming back

Why do you hold on
to the ones who don't care for you?
They left you at the wrong time
and watched you fall apart.
Your love may be true
but they didn't deserve it.
Pick up your broken pieces darling
you are the only one
who can save you.

Don't pretend to be sorry

You weren't there for me when I needed you
and I don't expect you to be, now
don't pretend to be sorry
for everything you have done.
Now you need something from me,
go right back to where you came from.

Ungrateful

The sun is shining but not that girl,
she sits on the steps and watches the world.
She was let down by everyone that she loved,
was that not enough to be so dull?
She'd always found pleasure in helping people.
Little did she know that they were going to be ungrateful.
If she could only stop, it would do her wonders,
unburden her from all the stress she is under.

Broken pieces

You heard a massive crash
You rushed into the room to see
the broken pieces scattered around.
For all the lies that you've told
you don't deserve me anymore.
My love was never yours
I'll fix my broken heart on my own.

Change yourself first

You silently wished for the world
to be a better place
but darling don't you realize
you can become better than them?

It will be okay

Mistakes were made
words went astray
nothing went right
it was a disappointing day.
But don't take it to heart
for tomorrow is another day
when things will go your way.

Deep Breaths

When you feel like you want to let go of
faith and dreams
friends and love,
when you want to be alone
away from ramblings and noise,
when the universe presses you down
and you want to let it crush you,
close your eyes
and take deep breaths
loosen your fist
and let the air flow
through your chest.

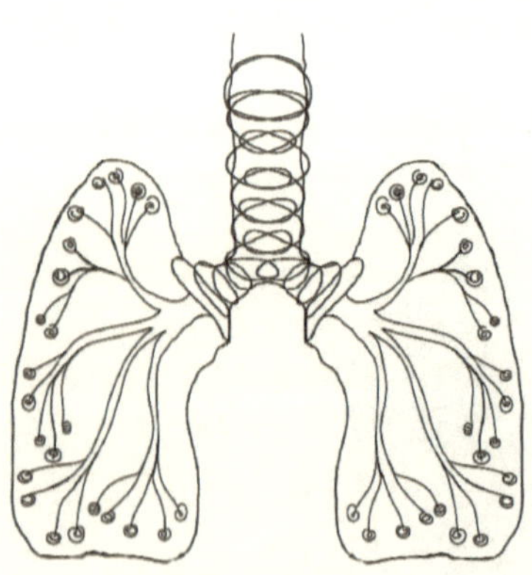

You're not the only one

I'm sorry if it's the first time you're hearing this
and nobody has ever hinted it before
we all have scars waiting to fade,
histories to move away from,
regrets we remember till date.
Each of us carries burdens
on our shoulders and backs
So, you're not the only one
who's going through this.

Imperfections

Don't shun away the emotions
just because they feel awful.
Let the guilt encompass you
make you realize what you have done.
You are not alone
your imperfections aren't your own.
They belong to everyone else
as we all rock on the same boat.
We fight, we hurt, we blame
and we all try to escape from this pain.
The only way to blossom
is to understand all the lessons we've gained
and to not repeat the mistakes
ever again.

Walls you've built

There are high concrete walls
decorated in graffiti and words of profanity.
Passers-by walk without a glance
I see your terrified eyes peeping
"Is it safe to come out now?"
Darling, I'll break down the buildings for you
So let me in
We'll fight together, it won't last
Help me break down your walls.

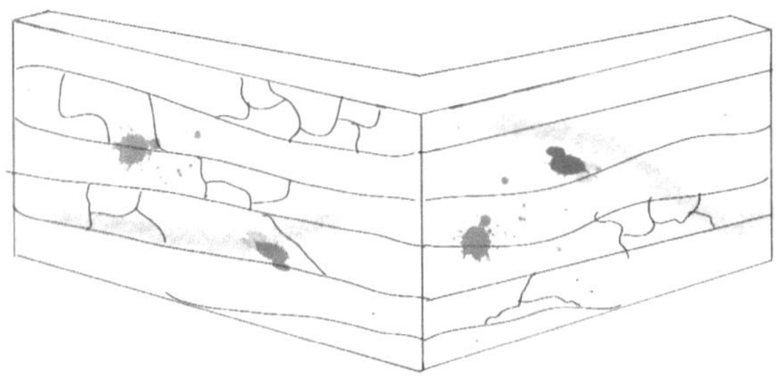

Baggage

I know I have to move on
from the parts of life
that have bothered me so much.
Moving on is not forgetting them
but placing all the baggage
lightly next to me
so that I can stretch my tired muscles.

Don't Resign

How will you do it
if you don't believe in yourself?
You have flaws
and failures too
but don't be blind to how much you are worthy.
Give yourself a chance
a second, a third
it's always better to try again
than to let yourself resign.

Brighter on the Other Side

Whatever struggles you're dealing with right now
know that they won't last
there will be bad days
but you'll grow through the darkness
and fight your storms.
When you're done
you will find it brighter
on the other side.

3. Rising Above

POISON AND ANTIDOTE

Antidote

When you're truly upset
and feel distant from the world,
read some poetry
and silently observe,
you're not going through this alone
your pains have been written in words.
The message and inspiration
will be therapeutic in verse
and help you accept
that this is just another phase.
The antidote to a broken life:
breathe the words of poetry
and help yourself revive.

Waves and Tides

Beyond the horizon,
is the vastness of the sea;
a collection of thoughts
and floods of dreams.
There are better days
that lie ahead,
unknown destinations
and dreams to realize.
We'll learn to
battle the tsunami of waves
brave the hurdles
that we'll face
and honor the words
of promises we make.

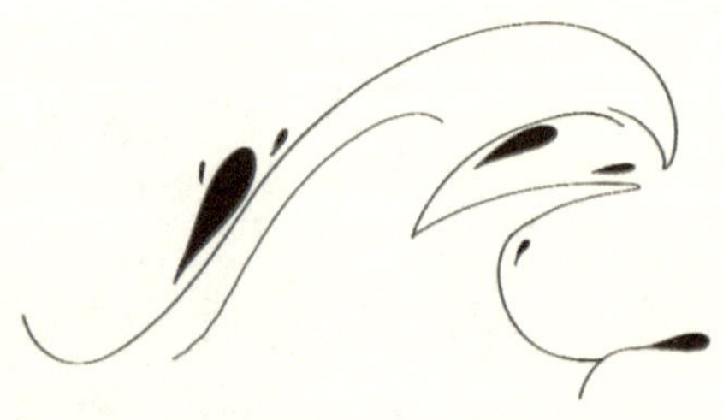

Ladder of Life

Life is a ladder, a series of rungs,
a different one for each person.
Yours may be wood or gold
but everyone has the same destination,
to reach the top.

Some people may pull you down
to make it seem like they're higher,
but you should continue your journey
because it's your strength that matters.

There will be people
who will push you to go further,
motivate you to do your best.
When you finally achieve your dreams
don't forget to lend a helping hand
when they're in need.

Of course, you may take some rest
or retrace a few steps back,
to look back at mistakes

and learn from the past.
And with the experience you have gathered,
you'll know exactly what to do
when you find a couple of rungs missing,
Climb on over or build them anew.

It might be easy to escape from troubles
as simple as letting go of those rungs,
but what matters in the end
is how far you have come
how much you have done
to make your life, worthy and content.

Wings

Don't look down
if you are afraid of heights
just close your eyes
put on your wings
I'll hold you tight.
You'll see there is nothing
to be scared of.
I'll help you fly.

Not giving up

I've done this too many times
to give it up now.
There has got to be a way
I've just got to find out how.
Others have gone through this before
I'm not alone.
If they can figure this out
I can do too.

Slow down

Take it one day at a time
there's no need to rush
It's okay to take it slow
one foot after the other
is more than enough.

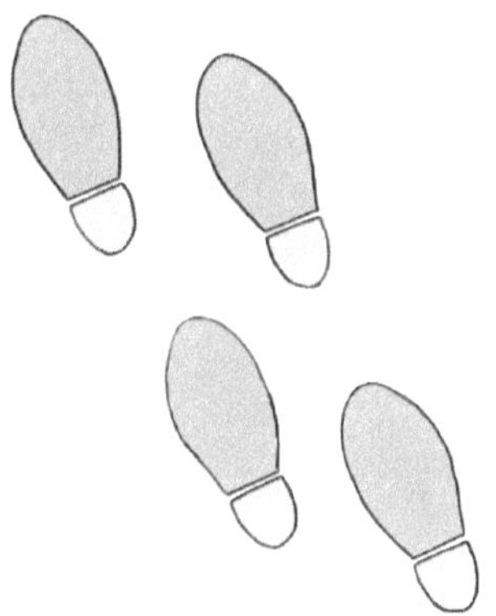

Self-compassion

Be gentle with yourself
you know you are hurting.
Treat yourself with kindness
you know you can use it.
Give yourself a break
you truly deserve it.
You owe it to yourself
to let your soul heal.

Buds

When they were just buds
picturing their blossoms
there was a glow within them
that was called innocence.
They worried not
about the storms or floods
They danced with the breeze
and had their fun.
But when the thunder struck
directly at their roots
they were absolutely rattled
down to their core.
Nothing could have prepared them for that
their time was over
they faded and dried away.
The sun rose the next day
and the rain watered her tears
on the withered plant.
And in its place
there rose a new baby bloom
that began spreading its new roots.

Poison apple

I bit the apple
of the poisoned tree
because they dared me to.
There were no seven dwarfs to save me
they thought they made me a fool.
They didn't realize
I wasn't Snow White.
All these years of accepting pain
has made me rise above their disdain.

Will power

She didn't look back
all the hate fell on deaf ears
She didn't stop once
her legs only took her forward.
When she reached the peak
she knew without a doubt
if she could do it all over again
she really would.

Hope on a Sunrise

When the cold night fades away
and the sun rises like every other day,
the rays give me the strength I need
to face my life, the rest of the way.

Trust yourself

Let me help you realize
what pain you're in.
Darling, I can see through your guarded skin
the scars and burns you keep hidden beneath.
Let me help you heal
and become stronger than you were.
You have faced the consequences
of many wrong choices
since you couldn't trust yourself.
But know that you can.
It's only a matter of when.
And when you do
your healing will begin.

Don't lose hope

Every day is unpredictable
but that's how it's supposed to be.
You battle through the odds
even when hope isn't anywhere to be seen.
People will stomp you
and drag you down
but it's your duty
to get back up
and stand tall.

So can you

Maybe it's too late for me
it doesn't have to be for you.
I've made too many mistakes,
things I can't undo anymore.
But I have learnt from them
and so can you.

Freeway

Life's a freeway
everyone is on their own paths.
If you've made some friends
you may take them with you
but if you've got no one
you must go alone.
If you're so focused on winning
and reaching the destination
then nobody will be by your side
when you're standing at Death's door.
Take life slowly
one day at a time,
make new friends along the path
and appreciate every moment of your life.

Collection

Collect every experience you find
keep them locked inside your heart
because you never know when
or where you might need them.

Life gives you lessons

I'm not sorry to see you go now
because I know you were here for a reason.
Life gives you lessons to learn
and you were one of them
for a short duration.

Liberation

There is a heaviness in my heart
as I think of what to say
It's scary and uncomfortable
but this isn't something I can escape from
No one will back me up
I have to do this myself
I must say what's on my mind
because I cannot hold it back anymore.

Who's the Victim?

There are heartless beings
who don't feel the need to care.
They hurt who they want
and play the victim in the end.
In the name of friendship
they take advantage of you.
Don't be fooled by these people
who wear fake masks everywhere.

Bullying

It's a bunch of people's words
against your own voice.
You've got to brace yourself
like you're getting ready for a fight.
Don't stand down
until you've had the last word.
They have got their insecurities
and have no right to put you down.
Speak up when it's needed
or you'll lose your own voice.

4. Peace Within

Phoenix

I'm rising from the ashes
stronger than before
The same fire that destroyed me
will burn me no more.

A New Beginning

Unlock yourself unto the world
you've been holding on for too long.
Close your eyes and take a deep breath
now let it all go.
Let all your sins fade away
begin anew from today.
Throw open the doors and let the breeze in
be proud of yourself and let that feeling sink in.
Get out of your shell and go for a walk
you might find everything you've been looking for.

Devil and Angel

I held hands with the devil
impressed with her regal bearing
her hands were cold
as she held mine tight.
I could tell what she was thinking
in her mind's eye.
She showed me events
from my entire life,
events when I had failed
despite my hard work
crashed my dreams
and let go of faith within,
events when I was at my worst
and didn't reach out for help
wallowed in my sorrow
ignoring everyone else,
events when I had given up
on the tasks at hand
instead of giving myself
a second chance.
I felt a hand on my shoulder
and as I turned around
in front of me there stood

a beautiful angel.
She pushed away the devil's hand
smiling, she took mine in hers
she looked deeply into my eyes
reassuring me everything was fine.
She said, "Darling, what you saw
surely makes you upset.
But that's what will fuel you
to do your best.
Some things are hard
but that's okay
because everyone has
both light and dark inside them
that they have to embrace.
All you have to do
is try again
push a little more
but be gentle with yourself.
Your true happiness
is when you forgive your past self.
The key to calm
your restless heart
lies within you
and nobody else."

Roots

My roots remind me of who I am
for without them I lose my identity
They keep me stable and poised
and in return I water them daily.

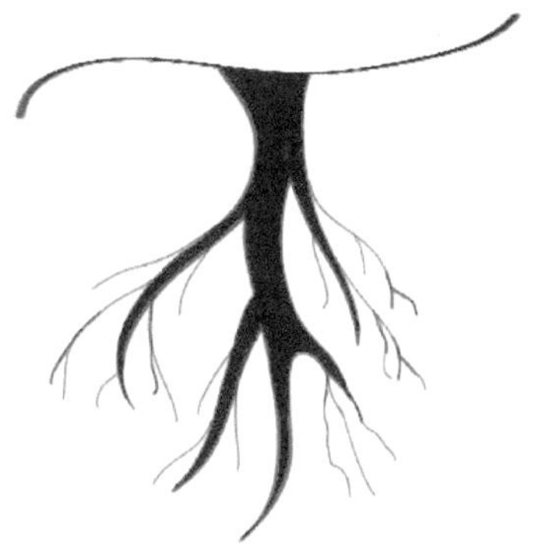

Love yourself

It's okay to put yourself first
it's okay not to care about others sometimes
Why would you want to,
if they don't care in return?
Love yourself
before anyone else,
the rest can come later.

Your potential

Love yourself
for who you can be
to the best of your abilities.

Within you

It's easy to lose yourself
in the chaos of this world
It's easy to get stranded
in a room of darkness.
Whatever peace you are searching for
lies within you.

Inner voice

Can you hear the whispers
that's coming from within?
It needs silence to find its voice
it's nudging you to listen,
"You are enough."

Changed

You loathe your past self
for making mistakes
but now you are not who you were
it's time to be proud of yourself.

Becoming whole

A piece of me was missing
somewhere in the distance.
I knew I had to go find it.
It took me several days
but in the end, it was worth it.
So let me tell you about my journey
the journey of finding myself
and learning to pave my own way.
I went far and wide and to beautiful lands
but I couldn't find what I was looking for.
I asked and searched and looked all over
but there were no fragments of myself around.
I had a compass but I thought it was broken
because it kept pointing in the direction that I had come.
In the course of time, I soon realized
that I had really lost my way
but I didn't want to give up and I pushed on,
I tried to have faith.
When I reached my inadvertent destination
I realized that I was back to where I had started.
After all those wonderful places I had been to
my missing piece was waiting for me
on the path that led back home.

Reflection

You point out my imperfections
like you have none.
Darling, what you see
is only a reflection.

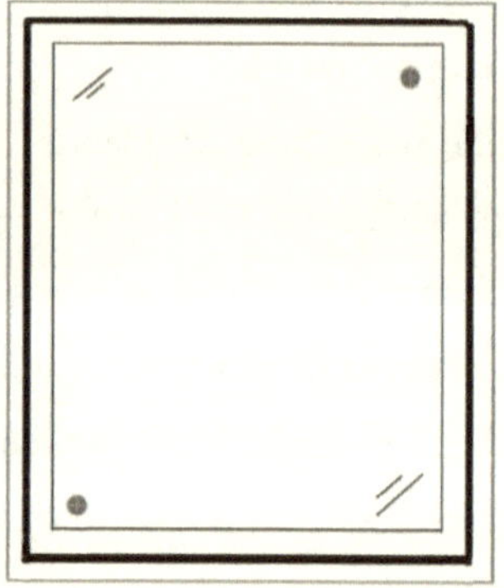

Leaving You

It became easy to love myself
once I left you
since you were holding me back
from being who I truly was.

Burning Bridge

I leave my worries behind me
as I watch the fire dazzle.
The heaviness in my heart
gravitates towards the ground
as I walk away from the burning bridge.

Lost and Found

There are days
when we lose our way
without a map in hand
or a vision in mind.
There are days
when our thoughts are absent
our heart, restless,
leaving us feeling exhausted.
And there are days
when we are in the dark
and that's okay.
Because there are days
when we reclaim ourselves,
tell our hearts
to look for what we've lost
because in the end
self-love is finally what we want to find.

Better ending

To all the people we tried to please
when we were young
and to make friends with,
your ego was bigger than your heart.
You looked at me like I was nothing
but now I look at you and laugh.
I realized that some things
are better when they end.
I'm in a better place than you
because I was true to myself.

Photo Album

I have memories
where my heart lies.
A faded photo album
resides within my depths.
The deeper I go,
the harder it is to get out.
As I unravel every page,
pictures and figures talk to me
and tell me the stories of long ago.
There is darkness and beauty
in between the lines
and when I finally reach the end,
it quotes,
"In loving memory of my future self,
look at you now."

Samyukta Balasubramanian is currently pursuing Computer Science Engineering in Bengaluru. She's an avid book reader and her favourite genres are fantasy, romance and contemporary. She is also interested in pencil sketching and has recently taken up digital art. She enjoys dancing and listening to music and has learnt Carnatic music. Writing has always been a part of her life since she was young. In her free time, she loves expressing herself through prose and poetry. She has also shared her work on Instagram (@pristine_poem).